SPECIAL OPS

The Takedown of Osama bin Laden

WANTED

by Natalie Lunis

Consultant: Fred Pushies
U.S. SOF Adviser

BEARPORT
PUBLISHING

New York, New York

Credits

Cover and Title Page, © U.S. Navy/Mass Communication Specialist 3rd Class Blake Midnight, Chris Whittle/Splash News/Newscom, U.S Navy/Mass Communication Specialist 2nd Class John Scorza, and U.S. Navy/Petty Officer 2nd Class Joshua T. Rodriguez; 4, © Visual News Pakistan/SIPA/Newscom; 5, © Ted Carlson/Fotodynamics.com; 6, © Masatomo Kuriya/Corbis; 7, © U.S. Air Force/Tech Sergeant Cedric H. Rudisill; 8L, © Balkis Press/ABACAUS/Newscom; 8R, © Chris Whittle/Newscom; 9, © AFP/Getty Images; 10, © AP Photo/Doug Mills; 11, © Russell Boyce/Reuters /Landov; 12, © Reza/Getty Images; 13, © Simon Klingert/ZUMA Press/Newscom; 14, © U.S. Air Force; 15, © Robin Nelson/ZUMA Press/Newscom; 16, © DigitalGlobe/Reuters /Landov; 17L, © Bettmann/Corbis; 17R, © AP Photo/Charles Dharapak; 18, © U.S. Navy/Petty Officer 2nd Class George R. Kusner; 19, © U.S. Navy; 20, © Pete Souza/White House/EPA/Landov; 21T, © U.S. Air Force/Paul Ridgeway; 21B, © Gary Fabiano/Sipa Press/Newscom; 23, © EPA/Landov; 24, © AP Photo/ Gene J. Puskar; 25, © Bay Ismoyo/AFP/Getty Images; 26–27, © Kevin Lamarque/Reuters/ Landov; 28TL, © Ted Carlson/Fotodynamics.com; 28TR, © Ted Carlson/Fotodynamics.com; 28B, © U.S. Marine Corps/Gunnery Sgt. James Frank; 29TL, © BankingBum; 29TR, © Rex Features via AP Images; 29BR, © Reuters /Landov; 29BL, © KrisfromGermany.

Publisher: Kenn Goin
Editorial Director: Adam Siegel
Creative Director: Spencer Brinker
Design: Debrah Kaiser
Photo Researcher: James O'Connor

Library of Congress Cataloging-in-Publication Data

Lunis, Natalie.
  The takedown of Osama bin Laden / by Natalie Lunis ; consultant, Fred Pushies.
      p. cm. — (Special ops)
  Includes bibliographical references and index.
  ISBN-13: 978-1-61772-459-6 (library binding)
  ISBN-10: 1-61772-459-9 (library binding)
  1. Bin Laden, Osama, 1957-2011—Death and burial—Juvenile literature. 2. United
States. Navy. SEALs—Juvenile literature. 3. Terrorists—Biography—Juvenile literature. 4.
Terrorism—Juvenile literature. I. Pushies, Fred J., 1952- II. Title.
  HV6430.B55L86 2012
  958.104'6092—dc23
  [B]

                                                2011040472

For more information, write to Bearport Publishing Company, Inc., 45 West 21st Street, Suite 3B, New York, New York 10010. Printed in the United States of America in North Mankato, Minnesota.

10 9 8 7 6 5 4 3 2 1

Contents

Swooping In

The dark early morning of May 2, 2011, was a quiet time in Abbottabad (uh-BOT-uh-*bod*), a small, pleasant city in northern Pakistan. Then, shortly after midnight, two helicopters moved in and swooped down on a house in a tree-lined neighborhood. This home was not like the others. It was larger and had a small separate guesthouse. Both of these buildings were mostly hidden behind a set of high maze-like walls.

The house in Abbottabad was about eight times larger than those in the rest of the city.

As each helicopter reached the ground, a group of American fighters spilled out. Soon, loud blasts filled the air. The **commandos**—all members of a group known as the Navy SEALs—blew apart walls and doors as they shot their way into the **compound**. Moments later, they entered the main house. Once inside, the SEALs were closer than ever to carrying out their mission—to hunt down the world's most wanted **terrorist**, Osama bin Laden.

One of the helicopters—an MH-60 Black Hawk like the one shown here—crashed as it tried to land. Luckily, the SEALs inside were not harmed and continued on with their mission.

"SEAL" stands for sea, air, and land. Navy SEALs are sailors who are trained to carry out missions in all these environments.

This map shows the location of Abbottabad, the city where the SEALs' raid took place.

September 11, 2001

How had Osama bin Laden become the world's most wanted terrorist? On the morning of September 11, 2001, at 8:46, an airplane carrying 92 people flew into one of the twin towers of the World Trade Center in New York City. Then, at 9:03 A.M., another airplane, this one carrying 65 people, flew into the other tower.

Fuel from the planes caught fire after the crashes, causing the twin towers to burn and then collapse.

By 10:30 A.M., both towers had burst into flames and collapsed. By the end of the day, military and law enforcement officials had learned that the two planes had been **hijacked** by terrorists as part of an attack on the United States. The terrorists were members of a group called **Al Qaeda**, which was led by a man named Osama bin Laden.

About 3,000 people died as a result of the terrorist attacks on the United States on September 11, 2001.

Two other planes were also hijacked by Al Qaeda terrorists on September 11, 2001. The hijackers crashed one of the planes into the Pentagon (shown above) in Washington, D.C., killing 184 people. The other plane crashed into a field near Shanksville, Pennsylvania. Forty people were killed.

Earlier Crimes

Before September 11, 2001, most Americans had never heard of Osama bin Laden. However, law enforcement officials, **intelligence agents**, and military leaders already knew a lot about him. In fact, bin Laden had already been on the **FBI**'s Ten Most Wanted list for two years.

Osama bin Laden's father became very wealthy by running a construction business in Saudi Arabia. After his father died, bin Laden (shown here) used money he inherited to pay for terrorist training and terrorist attacks.

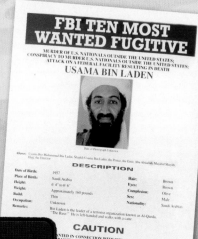

FBI TEN MOST WANTED FUGITIVE

MURDER OF U.S. NATIONALS OUTSIDE THE UNITED STATES;
CONSPIRACY TO MURDER U.S. NATIONALS OUTSIDE THE UNITED STATES;
ATTACK ON A FEDERAL FACILITY RESULTING IN DEATH

USAMA BIN LADEN

Aliases: Usama Bin Muhammad Bin Laden, Shaykh Usama Bin Laden, the Prince, the Emir, Abu Abdallah, Mujahid Shaykh, Hajj, the Director

DESCRIPTION

Date of Birth:	1957		
Place of Birth:	Saudi Arabia	Hair:	Brown
Height:	6' 4" to 6' 6"	Eyes:	Brown
Weight:	Approximately 160 pounds	Complexion:	Olive
Build:	Thin	Sex:	Male
Occupation:	Unknown	Nationality:	Saudi Arabian
Remarks:	Bin Laden is the leader of a terrorist organization known as Al-Qaeda, "The Base." He is left-handed and walks with a cane.		

CAUTION

WANTED IN CONNECTION WITH THE AUGUST 7, 1998, BOMBINGS OF THE EMBASSIES IN DAR ES SALAAM, TANZANIA, AND NAIROBI, KENYA. THESE TWO BOMBINGS KILLED OVER 200 PEOPLE. IN ADDITION, BIN LADEN IS A SUSPECT IN OTHER TERRORIST ATTACKS THROUGHOUT THE WORLD.

IF YOU HAVE ANY INFORMATION CONCERNING THIS PERSON, PLEASE CONTACT YOUR LOCAL FBI OFFICE OR THE NEAREST U.S. EMBASSY OR CONSULATE.

REWARD

The United States Department of State is offering a reward of up to $25 million for information leading to the apprehension or conviction of Usama Bin Laden. An additional $2 million is being offered and funded by the Airline Pilots Association and the Air Transport Association.

www.fbi.gov

The crimes that put Osama bin Laden on the FBI's list of ten most wanted **fugitives** occurred in other countries, but they were carried out against American citizens.

In August 1998, bombs went off in U.S. **embassies** in the East African countries of Kenya and Tanzania (*tan*-zuh-NEE-uh). More than 200 people, including 12 Americans, were killed. The same year, bin Laden was charged with murder in a U.S. court in connection with the bombings.

In October 2000, a powerful bomb ripped open the USS *Cole*, a U.S. Navy ship docked in the Middle Eastern country of Yemen. Seventeen American sailors were killed. Once again, **evidence** gathered by American investigators linked bin Laden and Al Qaeda to the attack.

Rescue workers try to save victims of Al Qaeda's bombing of the U.S. embassy in Kenya.

This map shows where bin Laden carried out some of his terrorist attacks before September 11, 2001.

The World's Biggest Manhunt

The hunt for Osama bin Laden did not begin on September 11, 2001, but as of that day, it became the biggest manhunt in the history of the United States. About 12 hours after the attacks, President George W. Bush appeared on television and pledged to take action. He said that he had told U.S. intelligence and law enforcement officials to do everything possible "to find those responsible and bring them to justice."

George W. Bush served as president of the United States from 2001 to 2009. He is shown here at the site of the World Trade Center, just three days after it was attacked.

After September 11, more than 7,000 FBI agents worked on the investigation into how the attacks were planned and carried out.

In the days that followed, government officials became more and more certain that Al Qaeda and bin Laden were behind the attacks. They were also fairly certain that bin Laden had overseen them from Afghanistan—the country in which he had been hiding from the American justice system since 1999. The challenge the **experts** now faced was how to track him down.

A few days after September 11, President Bush expressed his feelings about Osama bin Laden by describing a poster from the Old West that said "Wanted: Dead or Alive." Many people in New York shared these feelings—and some had this poster made and put on display.

Searching in Afghanistan

Afghanistan was the perfect hiding place for Osama bin Laden. Much of the country is made up of hard-to-reach mountains that have deep caves inside them. Also, since 1996, the country had been under the control of the **Taliban**. Like bin Laden, this group held extreme and strict views about **Islam** and thought of the United States as an enemy.

This cave in a mountain in Afghanistan was used as a hiding place by Osama bin Laden.

The Taliban not only offered its protection to bin Laden but also allowed him to run training camps for terrorists in Afghanistan. In 1998, the Taliban refused to turn bin Laden over to the United States after the attacks on U.S. embassies in Africa. In September of 2001, they again failed to hand him over after the attacks in the United States. As a result, the United States, joined by many other countries, sent troops to Afghanistan. The countries' goal was to fight terrorism and find bin Laden—dead or alive.

Together, the countries that went to war against terrorists in Afghanistan were known as the **coalition** forces. The group was led by the United States and included troops from more than 40 other countries.

The official name of the military action in Afghanistan was Operation Enduring Freedom. It was the first part of an effort that came to be known as the war on terror.

A Near Miss

In November 2001, coalition troops fighting in Afghanistan were closing in on Osama bin Laden. They knew the terrorist leader was hiding in a **network** of caves known as Tora Bora. From the air, the United States-led forces bombed the caves, causing heavy damage. At first, military leaders hoped that bin Laden had been killed during the bombing. However, in December, they learned that he had escaped.

U.S. forces used B-52 bombers, such as this one, to try to destroy the places where Osama bin Laden was hiding.

Most experts believed that bin Laden was now hiding somewhere near the border between Afghanistan and Pakistan. Despite a $25 million reward for information that would lead to him, however, the trail went cold. For almost ten years, no one hunting for bin Laden knew where he was. Then intelligence and military leaders came upon the breakthrough they were looking for.

The Navy SEALs and other **special operations forces**, such as the Army Rangers, Green Berets, and Air Force Combat Controllers, have been an important part of the fight in Afghanistan and the war on terror.

These Army Rangers were among the first troops to fight in Afghanistan following the attacks on the World Trade Center.

A New Lead

Over time, American investigators had been collecting information about people who were helping Osama bin Laden. One of them was a **courier** who had sometimes met face-to-face with the terrorist. By carefully following him, they discovered a large compound in Abbottabad, Pakistan. Among the people who lived there was a very tall man who always stayed hidden behind the high walls. Government officials knew that Osama bin Laden was about six and a half feet (2 m) tall. Could the tall man hiding in the compound be Osama bin Laden?

The U.S. government used photos like this one, taken from above, to learn about the compound.

Osama bin Laden's house

From August 2010 to April 2011, Leon Panetta, the head of the **CIA**, met with President Barack Obama and his top advisers to discuss the possibility that bin Laden had been found. Now the president had to decide how to act on the new information. He thought over different options military leaders had prepared. Then he approved one of the plans—a **raid** on the compound that would be carried out by Navy SEALs.

Before the raid, Navy SEALs studied maps and pictures of the compound to prepare for their mission. They also practiced the raid at a full-size model of the compound, which was specially built for them in North Carolina.

Barack Obama was elected president of the United States in 2008.

Military leaders considered bombing the compound from the air using a B-2 bomber like this one. However, the air strike would destroy Osama bin Laden's body if he was there. As a result, American officials would not know for sure whether they had killed the terrorist leader.

Send in the SEALs

President Obama and his top advisers knew that the plan the president had chosen—a secret raid during the middle of the night—was risky. However, they also knew that if anyone could pull it off, it was the Navy SEALs.

SEALs learn many special skills during their training. One of these skills is fast roping out of a helicopter—using a rope to quickly get out of the aircraft.

The Navy SEALs who were chosen to carry out the raid belonged to a special unit that some people call SEAL Team Six. The official name for the unit, however, is the Naval Special Warfare Development Group, or DEVGRU for short.

Because SEAL missions are usually carried out in secret, SEALs do not talk about their work. However, a few things about them are well known. For example, like members of other special ops units, SEALs are among the best-trained fighters in the world. They must stay in top physical shape, since their missions often involve dangerous activities, ranging from underwater diving to skydiving. SEALs also know how to work as part of a team and how to react quickly so that they are ready for any situation.

A variety of weapons play an important part in SEAL missions, and learning how to use them is an important part of SEAL training.

Watching from Washington

On May 1, just after 11:00 P.M., the SEALs were preparing to carry out their mission. Two MH-60 helicopters carrying the special ops team took off from an airfield in eastern Afghanistan. When they reached Abbottabad in the middle of the night on May 2, it was still the afternoon of May 1 in Washington, D.C. On that day, a group of people were gathered around a table in the **White House Situation Room**. Among them were President Obama, Vice President Joseph Biden, and **Secretary of State** Hillary Clinton. Everyone's eyes were fixed on a video screen.

The Situation Room in the White House has high-tech audio and video equipment. It is the place where top government officials can meet while keeping track of important events—such as the mission to take down Osama bin Laden.

On the video screen, Leon Panetta was speaking from another building—CIA headquarters in Langley, Virginia. He was receiving live images of the events that were taking place outside the compound in Abbottabad. He explained to the group in the White House what was happening. Once the SEALs entered the main house, however, no one but the special ops team could see what was taking place.

A military drone

Leon Panetta and other government officials were able to see what was happening outside bin Laden's compound because a drone, or pilotless aircraft, that had a camera attached to it was sending back images of the action.

Leon Panetta became the director of the CIA in 2009.

Inside the House

After entering the first floor of the house in Abbottabad, the SEALs looked for bin Laden in each room—but he was nowhere in sight. The SEALs then began to make their way upstairs in the three-story building when one of bin Laden's sons suddenly appeared. He began shooting at them—but the SEALs fired back and killed him. Still, there was no sign of bin Laden.

When the SEALs reached the top floor of the house, however, they saw a tall man with a beard peering out from behind a bedroom door. The commandos rushed into the room. They were now face-to-face with their target.

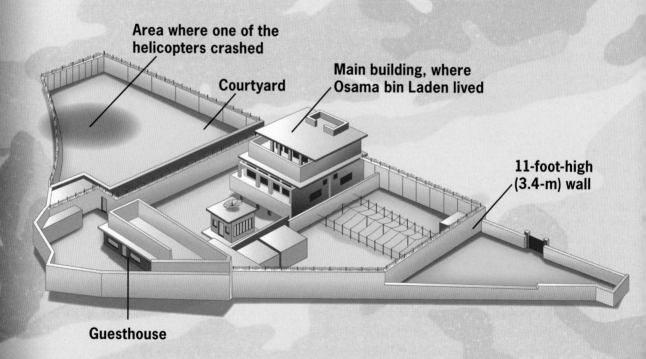

This diagram shows what the compound where the raid took place looked like.

The SEALs spotted two guns within bin Laden's reach. Immediately, one SEAL aimed his weapon at the terrorist. Firing one shot into his chest and one above his left eye, the SEAL killed Osama bin Laden.

The SEALs' work was not yet done, however. While some quickly gathered up paper **documents** and computers, others took steps to **identify** bin Laden's body. Then, about 38 minutes after hitting the ground, the SEALs took off into the air with the information and the body.

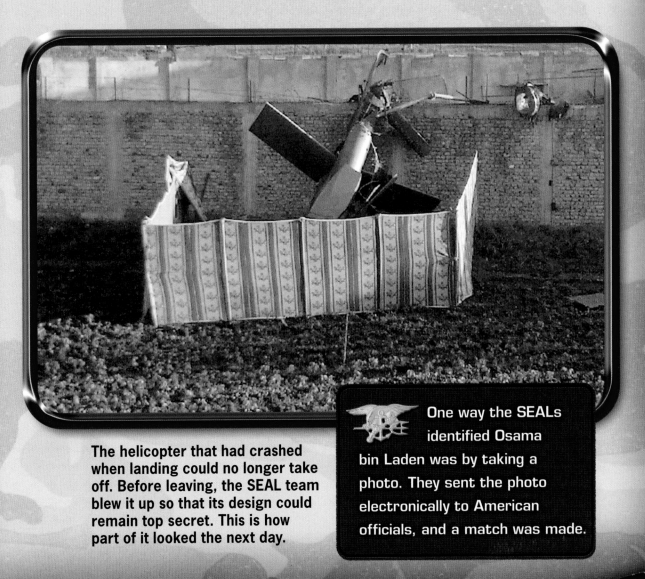

The helicopter that had crashed when landing could no longer take off. Before leaving, the SEAL team blew it up so that its design could remain top secret. This is how part of it looked the next day.

One way the SEALs identified Osama bin Laden was by taking a photo. They sent the photo electronically to American officials, and a match was made.

"Justice Has Been Done"

Everyone in the White House breathed a sigh of relief when a SEAL radioed and said four letters: "E.K.I.A." In the military, these letters stand for "Enemy Killed in Action." Once it was clear that the Navy SEALs had been successful, the top secret mission to hunt down Osama bin Laden was no longer a secret.

At the site of the crash in Pennsylvania, people attached newspapers with headlines about the mission's success to a fence.

None of the commandos were killed or injured during the raid on the compound. All returned from the mission safely.

On the night of May 2, President Obama gave a speech on television. In it, he recalled what had happened on September 11, 2001, calling it "the worst attack on the American people in our history." He also told about the events that led to the killing of the terrorist leader and stated that "justice has been done." In New York City, thousands of people gathered at the World Trade Center site to share their sense of pride and relief.

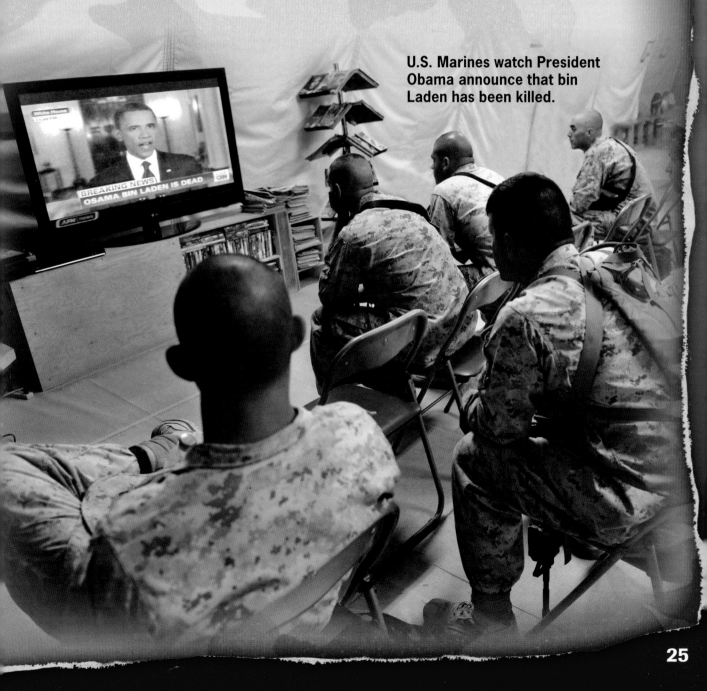

U.S. Marines watch President Obama announce that bin Laden has been killed.

The Mission Continues . . .

In the days and weeks following the takedown of Osama bin Laden, news stories revealed many details about the Navy SEALs' raid. People learned about the location and layout of the compound, the deliberate destruction of one of the helicopters, and the tense afternoon in the Situation Room of the White House.

Americans also learned a bit of information about the SEAL team that carried out the dangerous raid. For example, people learned that there were 23 SEALs on the mission and that they had a highly trained dog named Cairo (KYE-roh) with them. However, a great deal of information, including the sailors' identities, has not been revealed—and probably never will be. The secrecy helps protect the SEALs from enemies. It also allows them to continue to protect the United States—by sea, air, and land.

On May 6, 2011, at an Army base in Kentucky, President Obama met with some of the commandos who had carried out the raid, as well as other troops serving the country. He presented the commandos with the Presidential Unit Citation—the highest honor a military unit can receive.

During his visit, President Obama thanked the SEALs, as well as other troops who were gathered at the base, for "a job well done."

The Navy SEALs' Gear

Navy SEALs use lots of equipment to carry out their missions.

Here is some of the gear they use.

MH-60 Black Hawks The Navy SEALs used two of these helicopters to fly from an airfield in eastern Afghanistan to bin Laden's compound in Abbottabad, Pakistan.

MH-47 Chinooks Four of these helicopters were sent to wait a short distance from bin Laden's compound in case the SEALs needed extra help escaping during the mission. Two of the helicopters were waiting in Afghanistan, carrying 25 additional SEALs, and two in Pakistan.

HK416 The SEALs have not officially identified the weapon that killed bin Laden, but many experts believe that it was an HK416 like this one.

The SEALs brought these guns with them on their mission.

Sig Sauer P226 pistol

M134 Miniguns
Two of the Chinooks had this
kind of gun on board.

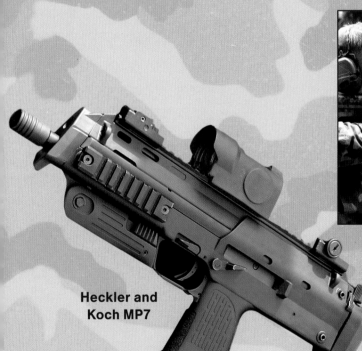

M4 rifle

**Heckler and
Koch MP7**

Glossary

Al Qaeda (*ahl* KAY-duh) the terrorist group that was responsible for the September 11 attacks on the United States

CIA (SEE EYE AY) abbreviation for Central Intelligence Agency; an American organization that gathers information in foreign countries for the U.S. government

coalition (*koh*-uh-LISH-uhn) a collection of groups that work together

commandos (kuh-MAN-dohz) fighters who use speed and surprise

compound (KOM-pound) a fenced-in area with buildings inside

courier (KUR-ee-ur) a person who carries messages

documents (DOK-yoo-muhnts) papers that contain information

embassies (EM-buh-seez) buildings that hold the offices of the representatives of other countries

evidence (EV-uh-duhnss) objects or information that can be used to prove whether something is true

experts (EK-spurts) people who know a lot about a subject

FBI (EF BEE EYE) abbreviation for Federal Bureau of Investigation; an organization that looks into violations of federal law for the United States Department of Justice

fugitives (FYOO-juh-tivz) people who are on the run from police or other law enforcement officers

hijacked (HYE-jakt) illegally took control of

identify (eye-DEN-tuh-fye) to tell who someone is

intelligence agents (in-TEL-uh-juhnss AY-juhnts) people whose job it is to collect and study information about an enemy

Islam (IS-lahm) one of the world's major religions; its followers are called Muslims

network (NET-*wurk*) a group of parts joined together, such as a group of buildings or tunnels

raid (RAYD) a quick surprise attack

secretary of state (SEK-ruh-*tair*-ee UHV STAYT) a high-level adviser who works closely with the president on matters having to do with other countries

Situation Room (*sich*-oo-AY-shuhn ROOM) a room in the White House with high-tech audio and video equipment, where top officials can meet to keep track of important events

special operations forces (SPESH-uhl *op*-uh-RAY-shuhnz FORSS-iz) groups of highly skilled soldiers in the military; called *special ops* for short

Taliban (TAL-i-ban) a military and political group that ruled Afghanistan from 1996 to 2001

terrorist (TER-ur-ist) a person who uses violence and threats to achieve his or her goals

White House (WITE HOUS) the building in Washington, D.C., where the president lives and works

Bibliography

The Editors of LIFE. *Brought to Justice: Osama bin Laden's War on America and the Mission that Stopped Him.* Des Moines, IA: LIFE Books (2011).

Mazzetti, Mark, Helene Cooper, and Peter Barker. "Behind the Hunt for Bin Laden." *New York Times* (May 2, 2011).

Schmidle, Nicholas. "Getting bin Laden: What Happened that Night in Abbottabad." *The New Yorker* (August 8, 2011).

Von Drehle, David. "Death Comes for the Terrorist." *Time* (May 20, 2011).

Read More

Greene, Jacqueline Dembar. *The 2001 World Trade Center Attack (Code Red).* New York: Bearport (2007).

Hamilton, John. *Operation Enduring Freedom.* Edina, MN: ABDO (2002).

Payment, Simone. *Navy SEALs: Special Operations for the U.S. Navy.* New York: Rosen (2003).

Yomtov, Nel. *Navy SEALs in Action (Special Ops).* New York: Bearport (2008).

Learn More Online

To learn more about Navy SEALs and the takedown of Osama bin Laden, visit
www.bearportpublishing.com/SpecialOps

Index

About the Author

Natalie Lunis has written many nonfiction books for children. She lives in New York's lower Hudson River Valley.